Reptile Keeper's Guide

ANOLES

R. D. Bartlett
Patricia Bartlett

BARRON'S

Acknowledgments

For assistance afield or in acquiring anoles to photograph, we extend our thanks to Carl Franklin, Billy Griswold, Chuck Hurt, Rob MacInnes, Walter Meshaka, Flavio Morrisey, Cesar Pena, Richard Reams, Dave Roberts, Dave Schleser, Brad Smith, Mike Stuhlman, and Kenny Wray. Special thanks are due our editor, Pat Hunter, for her thoughtful comments and assistance.

All inquiries should be addressed to:
Barron's Educational Series, Inc.
250 Wireless Boulevard
Hauppauge, NY 11788
http://www.barronseduc.com

Library of Congress Catalog Card No. 2001035648

International Standard Book No. 0-7641-1702-5

Library of Congress Cataloging-in-Publication Data
Bartlett, Richard D., 1938–
    Anoles : facts & advice on care and breeding /
    R.D. Bartlett and Patricia Bartlett.
        p. cm. — (Reptile keeper's guides)
    ISBN 0-7641-1702-5 (alk. paper)
        1. Anoles as pets. I. Bartlett, Patricia Pope, 1949–
    II. Title.
SF459.L5 B357 2001
639.3′548—dc21   2001035648

Printed in Hong Kong

9 8 7 6 5 4 3 2 1

Contents

Preface

My introduction to the wondrous world of anoles occurred nearly a half century ago when, as a child, I attended the New York Sportsman's Show with my parents. I can remember that in a gigantic coliseum there were aisle after aisle of all types of outdoor sports equipment—boats, tents, you name it—but the only thing I can still recall with clarity was a display of living "lapel lizards." Some were green, some were brown, and all, according to the salesman, were "American chameleons." Each wore a tiny collar and a neckchain with a small safety pin at the end.

I stood entranced, knowing even then that chameleons were famed for their color-changing ability and wondering whether these little lizards—which looked nothing like the chameleons I had seen in pictures—really could change their color. I didn't have to wonder long, for as I watched, one of those green lizards turned brown!

"Mom! Dad! Can I have some?"

The number I had hoped for turned out to be just one. As I left the Sportsman's Show I clasped a small traveling box with a cellophane window in the top. Inside was what I then thought was surely the most wonderful pet in the world—an American chameleon! The little reptile was accompanied by the most erroneous care instructions possible. We now know that despite their chameleon-like color changes, about the only things the anoles—for such were these lizards—have in common with the true chameleons is that both are lizards, both are primarily insectivorous, and both are largely arboreal.

Many of the lizards in both of these groups are capable of dramatic and rapid color changes. Because of this ability, some of the anoles are occasionally referred to as American chameleons. In fact, the two groups are not at all closely related. The anoles are fast-moving, streamlined New World

The long-snouted and angular Cuban green anole, *A. porcatus*, has recently colonized south Florida.

Down to its pinkish-red dewlap, the Cuban green anole is very similar to our native green anole in appearance.

This is a gravid female green anole.

lizards that have distended toe pads to help them climb smooth surfaces. They are far more closely allied to iguanas than to the chameleon. The chameleons are slow-moving Old World lizards with bundled toes, turreted eyes, and usually a strong prehensile tail like a watch spring.

After getting my anole home I removed its chain and collar, turned it loose in some houseplants, and watched in awe as it stalked and successfully caught insects as agile as houseflies. Although it did drink a little sugar water, it much preferred to lap droplets of water from the leaves of its houseplant habitat; anoles have been photographed returning repeatedly

to and drinking sweetened water from hummingbird feeders.

So, more by accident than intent, the lizard thrived. And for me that anole started an insidious progression of reptile- and amphibian-related questions and an interest that has never waned.

I don't think that anoles of any type are still sold at sportsman's shows. I do know that several species are now among the most common pet store lizards. Because they are relatively inexpensive, anoles are often an impulse purchase for beginning hobbyists. Unlike the real chameleons, anoles adapt readily to captivity and can live for years in simple caging with modest temperature controls. For these reasons, and because that first anole was my gateway into a world of herpetology, we wish to share some of our anole-related husbandry findings with those new to our hobby.

The yellow-edged orange dewlap is typical of the brown anole, *A. sagrei.*

Introduction

Green to brown, brown to green, and several shades in between. The common green anole is the only lizard species *native* to the United States that is capable of these dramatic color changes.

Anoles as a group, and the common green anole in particular, are so well known that an introduction to them seems almost unnecessary. Because they are active by day, they are readily observed, and because several of the species are entirely at home amid the habitat changes wrought by humans, anoles are often abundant in backyard settings.

The lizards in the anole grouping are subtropical to tropical lizards that have speciated widely in the West Indies and in the neotropics. Long considered a member of the huge and (then) unwieldy family Iguanidae, the anoles and their relatives are now contained in the family Polychrotidae. They are members of about six genera. There are more than 275 described anoles. It's likely that a few more are waiting to be discovered in tropical America.

Those anoles in the American pet trade are primarily species of the Bahamas, Cuba, the United States, and Guyana. Hobbyists in Europe (primarily in Germany) keep and breed many interesting species that are seen only rarely in America.

Male anoles are known for their distensible throat fans, which they use during territoriality and intimidation displays. The colors and patterns displayed on the throat fans are distinctive for each species, especially when you take into consideration that anoles are capable of seeing a greater range of light spectra than we do. Researchers have found that ultraviolet rays are reflected from the extended dewlaps, turning even the blandest throat fans into spectacular displays.

A male green anole sits atop a leaf.

Most anoles, including all of those seen with any regularity in the pet trade, are at least partially arboreal. Some are so strongly arboreal that they are considered canopy dwellers. Others spend much time only a few feet above the ground on fence posts, dwelling walls, or the trunks of trees. Those that inhabit ground surfaces and grass clumps are referred to as grass anoles.

Arboreal anoles have flattened, teardrop-shaped toe pads. Beneath these pads are great numbers of transverse grooves and ridges (lamellae), each of which contains bristlelike setae or hairlike projections that grip the slightest irregularities. These enable many species to climb a vertical glass pane, something to remember when setting them up in a terrarium.

In Europe, where anoles are coveted, difficult to procure, and expensive, captive-breeding programs have

The expanded toes of anoles are equipped with specialized structures that allow the lizards to climb both rough and smooth surfaces.

long been the rule. In the United States, where about a dozen species of anoles are still quite inexpensive, the pet trade depends mostly on wild-collected specimens.

Costs for pet anoles in the United States vary from $2 for brown anoles

This is a typical natural habitat for our native green anole.

Anolis chrysolepis scypheus of Amazonian South America is referred to as the yellow-tongued anole.

(*Anolis segrei*) to $5 for the common green anole (*Anolis carolinensis*). The very large and spectacular knight anole (*Anolis equestris*) varies in price from $15 to $35, according to availability. The interesting little anole relative known as the bearded chameleon anole (genus *Chamaeleolis*) is currently commanding upward of $500. Several types of bush anoles (genus *Polychrus*) are also occasionally available for the connoisseur. Prices for these range from $40 to $250 each.

Some species of anoles are inactive and a pair will thrive in a 20-gallon (76-L) terrarium. Others are very active and require a much larger terrarium to best survive in captivity.

In the following pages we will discuss the captive needs of about 10 of the more common forms (beginner species, if you will), but will mention three or four species more suited for the advanced collector. Small or large, inexpensive or costly, all of the polychrotines are immensely interesting and, as naturalistic terraria become more popular with hobbyists, so, too, do these hardy and intriguing lizards.

Huge knight anoles are now a common sight in Miami neighborhoods.

Although retained by females, the light vertebral stripe on this young male brown anole will disappear with age.

What Are the Anoles?

For the most part, anoles are alert, heliothermic (sun-basking), diurnal (active during the day), arboreal lizards that respond to approach by darting quickly to safety. Some of the most arboreal forms have perfected the technique known as "squirreling," which is sidling slowly around a limb or trunk to keep that obstacle between them and an approaching human in order to evade detection.

Most anoles are small, 5½ to 8½ inches (14–22 cm) in total length. The smallest are only about 4 inches (10 cm) long, and the very largest attain a length of only 18 inches (46 cm). Both extremes are now found in the United States, thanks to either accidental or purposeful introduction. All have long tails that autotomize (break off) easily and regenerate well along their distal half, but break less readily and regenerate more poorly closer to the lizard's body. Compared to the size of the eye opening in the skull, the eyes are rather small, but the lizard's vision is acute. All have well-developed legs, are capable of leaping considerable

Chamaelinorops barbouri of Haiti is a small and very slow-moving anole.

distances, and have expanded toe pads to assist them in climbing.

Many of the more arboreal forms (canopy dwellers) are capable of undergoing rapid and dramatic color changes. Those that dwell on trunks or limbs vary colors through a considerable range of grays and browns. A few may be blue in color or intricately and contrastingly patterned.

Let's take a closer look at about a dozen pet trade species of anoles.

Color-Changing Anoles

Green Anole
The natural range of the green anole, *Anolis carolinensis*, includes virtually all of the Gulf Coast and the south

A. sabanus is restricted in distribution to Saba and surrounding islets in the Lesser Antilles.

Atlantic states. It ranges inland as far as southeastern Oklahoma, southeastern Tennessee, and southern Arkansas. It has also been recorded in the Mexican state of Tamaulipas, and has become established in Japan.

Although highly arboreal, the green anole may occasionally be seen on the ground. Once common throughout its range, populations of this 5- to 8-inch-long (13–20 cm) anole have diminished in many heavily developed settings.

The color-changing abilities of the green anole are well known. An individual lizard may be brilliant green one minute and deep brown the next. These changes are triggered by stress, temperature, humidity, and light intensity, rather than the color of the lizard's background. If active, green anoles are often just that, a bright green; resting anoles are usually a deep brown. If involved in aggression, a green anole turns green with a black patch behind each eye. A lighter vertebral line is often present. Males are slightly larger than the females, and their tail base is heavier. Females may or may not have the pink throat fans, but their throat fans are much smaller than those of the males if they have them.

Cost for this species ranges from $2 to $5 each.

Cuban Green Anole

It was not until 1996 that science recognized a new species that had become established in Florida. This was the Cuban green anole, *Anolis porcatus*. From the breadth of its distribution in the greater Miami area, it seems apparent that this anole had been present in the state for many years, but it is so similar to the native common green anole that few people would differentiate the two. The Cuban green anole has larger cranial ridges than the common green anole, and the males of *A. porcatus* have a

Green anoles, *A. c. carolinensis*, easily ascend windowpanes.

light-edged dark spot immediately behind each foreleg. It is not known whether these two look-alike species can interbreed successfully. Both are of similar size and, to humans, at least, dewlap coloration is identical.

When it is differentiated from the look-alike common green anole, the cost of the Cuban species is between $10 and $15 each.

Knight Anole

The knight anole, *Anolis e. equestris*, a native of Cuba, was successfully introduced to Miami about a half century ago. This gigantic anole—males can measure up to 18 inches (46 cm), females a little smaller—is now a common sight throughout even metropolitan areas of this bustling city. It is usually a brilliant green color with two light yellow-to-white flash marks, one on the shoulder and one on the upper lip, from eye to ear opening. At times this lizard, often referred to as "iguana" in Miami, may be a deep

Some knight anoles raised in captivity are a bluish-green, perhaps due to a lack of beta-carotene or other color enhancing dietary component.

The knight anole may reach 18 inches (45 cm) in length, is very angular, and has a low serrate vertebral crest.

The gray dewlap is typical of the newly described pale-throated green anole, *A. carolinensis seminolus*, of southwestern Florida.

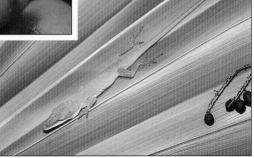

In the southeastern United States green anoles are often seen resting on palmetto fronds.

The Jamaican giant anole, *A. garmani*, is now established in southern and southwest Florida.

These lizards have a low crest of enlarged serrate scales down their back and a prominent nuchal (nape) crest. This species is persistently arboreal. It often hunts its insect prey while hanging from a tree trunk in a head-down position. It is very sensitive to cold; overnight temperatures of 40 to 45°F (4–7°C) may kill *garmani*.

This species is offered more infrequently than most others and may cost up to $75 each.

brown. The head is huge and strongly casqued, rising to a point at the back of the head. Throat fans are present on both sexes, with that of the male being proportionally larger.

This huge anole sells for as little as $20 and as much as $40 each.

Jamaican Giant Anole

The Jamaican giant anole, *Anolis garmani*, is now well established in southern Florida. Adult males often reach a foot (30 cm) in overall length; the females are somewhat smaller. Their generally brilliant green coloration may change to dark brown. Both sexes of the Jamaican giant anole have throat fans, but that of the male is larger and a brighter orange-yellow.

Quietly Colored Anoles

The color changes of many of the anoles that live low on tree trunks and in dried grasses are quite subtle. The very common brown anole, for example, varies from light to dark brown, but never assumes a green color. Many other of the tree trunk dwellers are hued similarly.

Brown Anole

The brown anole, *Anolis sagrei*, is a 5- to 8-inch-long (13–20 cm) species and was one of the first alien anoles to become established in Florida. It may now be south Florida's most

An occasional brown anole may be russet in overall coloration.

Introduced to Florida from the Bahamas and Cuba, the brown anole is now one of the most common lizard species in the United States.

The brown anole is the most terrestrial of Florida's polychrotine lizards. It may be seen nodding, bobbing, and distending its throat fan in territorial display in grasses, on sidewalks, and from clearing edges, as well as from brush piles, heaps of building debris, or from low on the trunks of trees and shrubs. Once acclimated, it will display in a terrarium.

Brown anoles usually cost less than $5 each.

Puerto Rican Crested Anole

Within the last few years the Puerto Rican crested anole, *A. c. cristatellus,* has gone from being a comparative rarity to being one of south Florida's most commonly seen lizards. Males are the larger—to about 7 inches (18 cm)—of the sexes, and are crested members of this species. Males have three interrupted crests, one on the tail, one along the back, and one on the nape. The nape and vertebral

commonly seen lizard species. It is also established in a few of central Texas's urban regions and the lower Rio Grande Valley.

The brown anole is able to exist both in high human population densities and in disturbed/modified landscapes, which pretty much describes Florida and central Texas.

Typical of most anoles, male sagrei are much larger than female sagrei, both in length and proportionate heaviness of body. The males are also the darker of the sexes in color, and are very feisty. The throat fan of the males may vary from yellow-orange to orange and has a whitish border. When not distended, the border of the throat fan forms a light streak on the throat of the male lizard. Some males have rather well-developed tail crests. In fact, some male brown anoles have *much* more prominent caudal cresting than the anoles named for their crests, the Puerto Rican crested anoles.

Male brown anoles are heavy-bodied and very alert.

Crested anoles, *A. c. cristatellus*, a Puerto Rican native, are now well established in Miami, Florida.

Adult male large-headed anoles are very wary and not easily approached.

crests are voluntarily erectile through muscle contractions. The caudal crest is always discernible, and is the one for which they are named.

This lizard varies in color from dark to light brown, and may or may not have darker body blotches. The tail is banded. The large throat fan of the male is pale yellow. Females look much like female brown anoles, having a dark-edged light vertebral stripe.

Crested anoles may cost up to $10 each.

Large-Headed Anole

Although it is known from only a few small colonies in south Florida, the evasive large-headed anole, *Anolis c.*

cybotes, seems to be holding its own. Adult males are among the most impressive of the smaller brown anoles. Adult males are a bulky and bigheaded 8 inches (20 cm) in length; females are a normally proportioned 5 inches (13 cm). This is a native of Hispaniola. Subtly colored, large-headed anoles are always some shade of brown, occasionally with vague olive overtones. They are often darkest dorsally, have two stripes, and may be dark banded as well. The very large throat fan of the male, yellow to buff in coloration, may shade to pale orange centrally when distended. Males are capable of erecting vertebral and nuchal crests. Female large-headed anoles are very similar in appearance to the females of the ubiquitous brown anole.

Large-headed anoles usually cost less than $15 each.

Bark Anole

Because of a diet that centers largely on arboreal ants, the little bark anoles, *Anolis distichus*, are poorly suited as pets. They are only about 4 inches (10 cm) in length, and may vary in color from pea green to warm brown. Their colors blend remarkably well with the barks of the trees on which they are found. All are indigenous to the West

Most bark anoles, *A. distichus*, in Miami have mustard yellow dewlaps.

The bark anole is the smallest of the Florida species and preys primarily on ants.

Indies. They are quick, agile, and, once alerted, adept at escaping predators. Males have a pale yellow dewlap.

Even at a cost of less than $5 each, we urge that bark anoles not be purchased.

Blue Anole

There are several other anoles that are occasionally available in the pet trade. One is an interesting bluish gray and olive green lizard called the blue anole. It is originally from Barbados, but now also hails from Guyana and Venezuela. The blue anole, *Anolis (roquet) extremus*, is an 8-inch-long (20 cm) species. It seems to be hardy and easily maintained, similar to a common green anole.

The cost of this species is usually less than $15.

Bearded Chameleon Anole

The foot-long (30 cm) bearded chameleon anole, *Chamaeleolis barbatus*, resembles nothing so much as a breathing piece of bark with eyes. Its pattern of light and dark markings on its gray body render this Cuban native almost invisible as it clings quietly to a shady branch or tree trunk. Even its dewlap is a combination of gray on gray, but if the lizard is disturbed, the vaguest blush of pink may suffuse the distended throat fan. The tail is stout and weakly prehensile. Compared to most anoline lizards, this (and the

This anole from Guyana is now thought to be a subspecies of *Anolis (roquet) extremus* that has been introduced from Martinique.

This is a small female bearded chameleon anole.

Polychrus marmoratus, the marbled bush anole of Amazonian South America, is available sporadically to hobbyists.

Polychrus acutirostris of southern South American savannas is commonly known as the sharp-nosed bush anole.

bush anoles, described a little further on) is comparatively slow moving. It feeds well on slugs and insects.

When available these lizards cost about $500 each.

Sharp-Nosed Bush Anole

The sharp-nosed bush anole, *Polychrus acutirostris*, dwells in the low shrubs where it balances on wind-blown twigs with its very long, slender, semiprehensile tail helping to stabilize it. This is a slender lizard that is occasionally imported from the seasonally rainy regions of Paraguay. Unless disturbed it moves slowly in a chameleon-like, hand-over-hand fashion.

When available this species costs about $100.

Marbled Bush Anole

The primarily green marbled bush anole, *Polychrus marmoratus*, is a tropical rain forest species that is occasionally found in the American pet trade. This lizard is beautiful, fairly slow moving, and quite hardy.

The cost of this anole is about $200.

Other Species

Specialty dealers occasionally import a few other anole species. One Cuban species is the blue and green Allison's anole, *Anolis allisoni*. It is remarkably beautiful. Other imported anole species are less impressive, being variations on a brown theme, but like other anoles, if provided a varied insect diet and kept well hydrated, they are very hardy and interesting terrarium lizards.

Anoles as Pets

Anoles of all kinds make ideal terrarium animals but, like many other lizards, don't take to being handled. To a species, they are rather nervous, and do not tolerate being restrained by a human hand. The stress they feel from physical handling can usually be easily seen in the color changes they undergo while being handled.

Requirements

Except for the green anole that ranges well up into the Carolinas, Tennessee, and Oklahoma, anoles are subtropical and tropical lizards of the New World. Whether they are kept indoors or outside, their requirements are basically the same. Their terrarium or cage must be kept warm—78 to 85°F (25–29°C) with a basking area of 95 to 98°F (35–37°C)—and relatively humid. The lizards must be supplied with ample amounts of the correct food and with drinking water. Captive anoles must be provided with adequate vitamin/mineral supplements, be lit with full-spectrum lighting (the sun will take care of this in outside cages), and they must be given sufficient physical space. Only a single male (but up to several females) may be kept in each cage, unless they are of very diverse species and each has a very different body language.

Most anoles are active lizards and do best if not crowded. Because of the diversity in species size, there necessarily will be a diversity in the size of the caging requirements. Illuminated and warmed horizontal and vertical perches for basking and displaying—many anoles preferentially position themselves head downward on vertical supports—must be incorporated into any cage design.

Many green anoles of the Florida Keys have a yellowish overlay of color.

Lighting

Why full-spectrum lighting? As we have mentioned, most anoles and many of their relatives are heliothermic lizards. That is, they bask in the sunlight both for warmth and to derive a complex array of health benefits from the ultraviolet rays—both UV-A and UV-B. UV-A promotes natural behavior; UV-B aids in synthesizing previtamin D_3, which in turn facilitates the metabolizing of dietary calcium.

UV can be derived from unfiltered sunlight or from full-spectrum bulbs. However, if the latter is used, the UV-producing bulbs should be no more than 10 inches (25 cm) away from the basking area, and most become markedly less effective after six months. If denied access to UV rays, the benefits derived from them must be provided in some other way. The most frequently used way is by supplying vitamin D_3 and calcium dietary supplements. This will be discussed more fully in the feeding section (page 30).

In addition to full-spectrum lighting, heating and illumination can be provided by strategic placement of low-wattage plant-grow floodlights.

Drinking

Being arboreal lizards, anoles generally drink droplets of dew and rain from the leaves and branches in which they dwell. They are slow to recognize a dish of still water as a drinking source, and some never do. Anoles as a group will readily lap water from broad-leafed live plants that are misted frequently, at least once a day. If water is provided in a dish, agitating the water's surface by using an aquarium airstone or, alternatively, a bubbler bowl (a commercially available bowl having a built-in airstone to roil the water) will enable most anoles to perceive that this otherwise ignored source has drinking potential.

Life Span of Anoles

Wild-caught adults of all species regularly exceed a four-year life span in captivity, and some have lived longer than eight years. The lives and activities of

The Puerto Rican giant green anole, *A. cuvieri,* is an uncommon species.

The Hispaniolan green anole, *A. chlorocyanis,* is another beautiful species that is capable of dramatic color changes.

Male anoles (this is a green anole) use a distended dewlap and other body language to deter other males from approaching.

these little lizards prove beyond any shadow of a doubt that herps neither need to be large nor exotic to be interesting and worthy of study.

Very few anoles, especially of the species found in the United States, are captive bred for the pet trade. The vast majority of the lizards seen in pet stores and on dealers' lists are collected from the wild. Or, if you are planning to vacation in Florida, perhaps you would prefer to collect your own? It can be done.

Obtaining Your Anoles

• Any anole that you select should appear active and alert, have all of its fingers and toes, not have open wounds, and not have sunken eyes.

Brown anoles often position themselves head downward, low on tree trunks.

• Whether you select one with a broken or regenerated tail will be largely up to you; neither is particularly serious, but keep in mind that an anole's regenerated tail is never as attractive or perfect as the original.
• Do not select an obviously undernourished anole—one with ribs starkly evident or with the pelvic girdle protruding—or one with loose stools or with feces smeared at the anal opening. Since most anoles found in the American pet market are collected from the wild, you may wish to have fecal smears done by a veterinarian to determine gutparasite type and load.

Anoles can be obtained in any of several ways. Some species may be available at neighborhood pet stores and others from specialty dealers. Many species can be found advertised on the Web or in the classified section of reptile magazines. Let's explore some of these avenues of acquisition.

Before purchasing your anole, have its caging readied. Large species such as the knight and Jamaican giant anoles will require larger caging than would be necessary for smaller species.

Green anoles may be green or brown in color.

Male crested anoles have orange-edged yellow dewlaps.

Pet Stores

We advocate purchasing your anoles at local pet stores when possible, where you can see the animals, discuss them freely with store personnel, personally assess the lizards' health, and watch them feed and interact. Some pet stores will special-order anole species for you.

Although they are favorites of the hobbyists, many species of anoles are so readily collected from the wild and so inexpensive that there is little incentive for herpetoculturists to develop breeding programs. It is a little different with some of the rarer species. These may be available only through captive-breeding programs, either here or in Europe.

The bearded chameleon anole, *Chamaeleolis barbatus*, a Cuban species, is becoming increasingly popular with hobbyists.

Specialty Dealers

Specialty dealers—vendors who deal directly with breeders and collectors across the world—may offer some beautiful and unusual species. These may also be advertised on the Web and in the classified sections of reptile magazines.

World Wide Web

Within the last few years the World Wide Web has become an important

source of information. By instructing your search engine to seek "anoles" or a specific kind of anole, you should learn of the status and availability of the creatures both in the United States and abroad.

Herpetological Clubs

Herpetological clubs also exist in many cities. You can learn about these by asking at pet stores, museums, college biology departments, or at some high schools. At these meetings, if queried, fellow enthusiasts may be able to offer comments about some reptile dealers.

Mail-order Purchase and Shipping

Even today, with expanded neighborhood pet stores now the norm, many of the most beautiful anoles are seldom locally available. If this is the case, mail order may be the answer. You may find the species you want on the Web or advertised elsewhere and elect to have it shipped to you, but ask a few questions at first. At the outset, seek pertinent answers about the anole's cost, feeding habits, age, and other statistics, then decide whether this is really the anole you want. If the answer is yes, the chances are excellent that the supplier is familiar with shipping and will be delighted to assist you in any way possible.

Among the things on which you and your shipper will have to agree is

Anolis (roquet) extremus, a native of Barbados and other Caribbean Islands, is occasionally seen in southwest Florida.

the method of payment and the method and date of shipping. The shipping is most safely accomplished when outdoor temperatures are moderate.

Lizards may be shipped in a number of ways. Discuss the pros and cons of each with your shipper. Today there is a growing tendency to use the door-to-door services of carriers such as USPS, UPS, and FedEx. These are less expensive and often faster than traditional airport-to-airport airline service. All methods will add an additional cost to the price of the anole. Discuss this and the method of payment with your shipper.

A blue dewlap and mouth-lining identify the Amazonian blue-lipped anole, *A. bombiceps.*

Shipping by any service on weekends, holidays, or during very hot or very cold weather may be difficult and should be discouraged. If applicable, pick up your shipment as quickly as possible after its arrival. This is especially important in bad weather. Learn the hours of your cargo office and whether the shipment can be picked up at the ticket counter if it arrives after the cargo office has closed.

Unless otherwise specified, reliable shippers guarantee live delivery. However, to substantiate the existence of a problem, both shippers and airlines will require a "discrepancy" or "damage" report made out, signed, and dated by the carrier's agents. Learn from your shipper exactly what he or she expects should a problem occur.

Collecting Your Own Anoles

Exactly how you would go about collecting your own anoles will depend on whether you are an opportunistic

This anole was described as *A. blanquillanus* by European researchers. It is native to a small group of islands north of Venezuela.

hobbyist or a dedicated herp collector.

It seems that at some point in almost everyone's life he or she visits the state of Florida. Only there can you find Florida's one native anole plus at least six other kinds. And if, while you're visiting the anole state, you look in the right places, such as in the proximity of reptile importers, you might find a few other "new" anole species.

Some hobbyists merely want a pair or two of green anoles or brown anoles—the two most widely spread and abundant species—if they happen upon them while on a Florida vacation. Other hobbyists actually create their vacations around the possibility of collecting exotic anoles as well as other reptiles and amphibians.

To do the latter, you'll need to go far south on the Florida peninsula. Your best place to find most of the exotics will be in the Miami area. Brown anoles can be readily found south of a line drawn from Tampa Bay to Melbourne and, with a little effort, far north of there. Green anoles can be found during the summer months in the lowland areas of our Gulf Coast and south Atlantic states.

Changeably Colored Green Anoles

Florida's single native anole species, the changeably colored green anole, may be encountered in both urban and woodland settings. Look for it by day as it suns on the boles of trees, telephone poles, garden fences, and other such areas. At night this species may rest on a low leaf or a blade of grass where it can be easily seen by flashlight.

In all but the perpetually warm areas of their range, green anoles become dormant during the months

Adult male crested anoles have a low crest on their tail.

of winter. They may be found year-round in much of Florida and the Lower Rio Grande Valley.

Cuban Green Anoles

It seems that in many areas of Miami, the very arboreal Cuban green anole has all but replaced the native common green anole. These two species are very difficult to differentiate, but males of the Cuban green usually have a black spot on each side, just behind the front legs; this is called a postapical spot.

Brown Anoles

The brown anole occurs both in natural and disturbed settings. Brown anoles are a "low to the ground" species that can be found in shrubs, on roadside signs, the lower trunks of trees, fences, trash piles, fallen limbs, and tree trunks—even the walls of sheds and houses. Like most anoles, the males are considerably larger than the females. Females often have a broad, light, middorsal stripe with gracefully scalloped edges. Males are darker than females and often have obscure dark markings. Males have a light-edged orange-red dewlap.

Bark Anoles

The little gray to pea green bark anoles are usually seen in Dade County in thickets of low shrubbery.

They are not uncommon near houses, but have expanded their ranges outward from urban areas along the canal systems. Tangles of bougainvillea, Suriname cherry, and crotons are favored habitats. Bark anoles are the smallest species of anole to yet become established in the United States. The pale yellow dewlap of the males and the dark dorsal chevrons of both sexes are diagnostic characteristics. Because of their predominantly ant diet, bark anoles can be difficult to keep.

Knight Anoles

During the summer months, knight anoles are common over much of Miami. They may be seen in head-down positions low on the trunks of broad-leafed trees. Their yellow shoulder markings and huge pink dewlaps (both sexes have dewlaps) render the lizards quite conspicuous. Remember that this big lizard can and will bite—hard.

Jamaican Giant Anoles

In some of the larger trees in Dade County you may find the Jamaican giant anole. Like the knight anoles, Jamaican giants seem to descend lower in the trees during the hot, humid days of summer.

Male large-headed anoles, *A. c. cybotes*, have a huge pale-yellow dewlap, a very large head, and some cresting on the body and tail.

A. capito is a very well-camouflaged ground dweller from Central America.

Puerto Rican Crested Anole

The Puerto Rican crested anole usually positions itself low on tree trunks, fences, trash piles, and so on in Miami and Coral Gables. The throat fan of this species is light yellow to very pale orange.

Other Species

At least four other species of anoles have been recorded from Florida: the large-headed, Hispaniolan green, Guyanan blue, and Marie Gallant crested anoles. Because they are present in only small numbers, often in very circumscribed areas and on private land, finding these will be more problematic.

Foreign Anoles

There are a large number of reptile dealers and importers in Miami who periodically market foreign anoles. Since anoles are agile and easily escape the cages in which they are placed when doors are opened, there is always the chance that you'll find an escapee of a species not previously reported. Not all anoles that escape live but, as we have seen, occasionally some do, and end up creating viable populations of alien herpetofauna.

Note: No license is necessary to collect alien reptiles for personal use in Florida. Existing laws can be checked with the non-game department of each state's Game and Fish Commission.

A. biporcatus is a large, color-changing, Central American anole.

Caging

Since many of the anoles in the pet industry are arboreal species, we prefer to provide them with vertically oriented caging. Many of the arboreal anoles are capable of assuming beautiful colors; some are even very interestingly patterned.

These beautiful lizards can be kept in intricate terraria, simple terraria, large wood and wire cages, or even suitably appointed greenhouses.

The Terrarium

Size

The size of their terrarium must be tailored to the size and number of the active lizards that are to be kept in it. Anoles do not tolerate crowding well over long periods. For a pair or trio of small to moderately sized anoles a 30-gallon (113-L) "tall" tank will provide sufficient space.

For a pair or trio of the large species, we suggest nothing smaller than a 50-gallon (189-L) tall terrarium; a larger one would be even better. If constrained too tightly, anoles may survive but won't thrive and there will be an unnatural amount of squabbling in a group. So, in all cases, the more room, the better.

Plants

It is best if broad-leafed plants of some type are included in the terraria. The little lizards will stretch out on the leaves to sleep. Larger anoles, such as the knight and Jamaican giants, will prefer to sleep on horizontal limbs of at least the diameter of their body.

Territoriality in the Terrarium

Male anoles avidly defend their territories against interlopers. In the case of small species, this involves about 4 feet (1 m) cubed; for large species it may include an entire treetop. However, the lizards often stray far beyond territorial boundaries. The territoriality displays include a lateral

A. b. bahorucaensis may have wide turquoise bands crossing its back.

This Jamaican giant anole peers from his terrarium foliage.

A very small population of Marie Gallant sail-tailed anoles, *A. ferreus*, exists in southwest Florida.

flattening of the body to make them appear larger, push-ups, head bobs, and distending the throat fan. A low, vertebral ridge may also be elevated. If this does not dissuade the interloper, the defending lizard will then sidle broadside toward the interloper, then dart toward and actually skirmish with the offender. The fights can be fierce, and will last until the interloper rushes off or the defender is deposed.

The feisty brown anole will display not only at others of its own kind but also at our dogs, and even at us. We can usually induce it to bob at us if, after making eye contact with the lizard, we animatedly bob *our* heads. The lizard will respond by bobbing, then distending its throat fan. Not having throat fans ourselves, we lose the argument.

Suggestions for a Large Movable Outside Anole Cage

Most anoles are heliothermic lizards that bask extensively. Whenever possible, we provide our animals access to natural, unfiltered sunshine. In the snowbelt states, anoles can be main-tained outside only during the warmest of summer weather. In the sunbelt, they remain outside for much more of the year.

Our large outside cages are made of wood and wire. Large casters are attached to the bottom to facilitate ease of cage movement. This allows us to easily move the cages to best utilize the sunlight and ambient temperatures.

Size
Our outside cages are large—72 inches high (including the casters) × 48 inches long × 32 inches wide (183 × 122 × 81 cm). The cages have a bottom and top of 3/4-inch (19-mm) exterior plywood and are framed with pressure-treated 2 × 2s. A 1/8-inch (3-mm) mesh hardware cloth is used for the wire because this prevents the escape of all but the smallest-size crickets.

The outside dimensions of the cage are tailored to allow it to be rolled inside through sliding patio doors if the weather changes. The dimensions of the hinged, front-opening door are 24 × 48 inches (61 × 122 cm). The wire is stapled to the frame using stainless staples from a standard, hand-powered staple gun. Those staples that don't set tightly are tapped in with a hammer.

Cage Furniture

Cage furniture in each cage includes a potted ficus tree or hibiscus bush, a number of diagonal and horizontal branches all 2 to 3 inches (5–8 cm) in diameter, and hanging pots of vining pothos. Several bags of potting soil, over which a substantial layer of dried leaves is added, are spread around the bottom of each cage. Although some of the substrate washes through the wire with each rainstorm or cage cleaning, it lasts for several weeks before it needs to be replaced. To thoroughly clean the cage, the lizards are removed, the uprights, top, and bottom are scrubbed with a dilute bleach solution (1 part bleach to 10 parts water), then the whole cage is washed thoroughly with a garden hose. New substrate is poured into place.

Heat

In the warmer states, the cold spells during the winter aren't severe. These substantial cages are covered with 6-mil plastic sheeting during the winter months. This is stapled firmly

in place over three sides and the top. The top sheet of plastic is fitted around an above-cage heat lamp; the bulb must not touch the plastic. The front of the cage is covered with a separate sheet of plastic that is stapled only at the top. This allows us to roll that side up to feed, water, and care for the animals, or to leave that side open when the weather is sufficiently warm.

This arrangement works well until outside temperatures drop below 45°F (7°C). Then we roll the cages indoors.

Greenhouses

Greenhouses heated during the winter and containing many broad-leafed plants are ideal year-round homes for anoles. There are many styles of greenhouses, made from all types of construction materials and formats, readily available today. These vary from simple, self-standing, fully constructed variations on the storage shed, through myriad do-it-yourself kits, to elaborate and decorative commercial models. These substantial commercial models are usually best left in the hands of a general contractor, unless you are very handy. Greenhouses with double glazing are

An aquatic anole? Indeed, *A. aquaticus* of Central America is one of several such species.

A Simple Terrarium for Anoles

A beautifully appointed anole cage can be made from a 65-gallon (246-L) hexagonal aquarium.

1. Illumination and warmth can be provided by an incandescent UV and heat bulb, directed downward through a wire mesh top.
2. Cage furniture can include a large, vertically oriented, hollow log, a few horizontal and diagonal basking branches, and growing plants such as pothos (*Epipremnum aureum,* also called variegated philodendron).
3. A feeding platform can be placed for the food dish or the mealworm dish. Crickets can just be dumped into the cage; the anoles will pursue them or just gobble them up as they wander by.
4. The substrate consists of several inches of sterilized potting soil, which contains a few earthworms to move the soil around and help keep it fresh. If properly illuminated, moistened, and not overcrowded, such an arrangement can go for several years between changes.
5. Eggs are generally laid on the substrate and can be gathered and moved to an incubator. Eggs that aren't found generally hatch on their own, and you suddenly see tiny replicas of the adults darting about.

Shape

A terrarium of standard shape will suffice equally well. Always remember that anoles of all species are talented escape artists. Their terrarium, whatever its shape, must be tightly and totally covered.

Tops

If your terrarium is oriented in a standard manner and is of a standard shape, covering it is a simple matter. Clip-on screen or wire mesh tops with either molded plastic or galvanized frames are readily available at many pet stores. Tightly covering your terrarium if it is an odd shape (hex tanks can be difficult to find covers for) or oriented vertically is more problematic.

A metal-framed wire top can be used for a vertically oriented terrarium. Raise the terrarium by placing it atop two 1 × 2 wooden strips. This makes it easy to snap the top on and off.

However, reptile tanks with built-in sliding screen tops are now readily available in many pet stores. These screen tops slide open and closed on molded plastic frames that are permanently affixed to the terrarium. The tops close tightly and are lockable. We consider these terraria an excellent choice for housing anoles.

Heat

If you use a heat lamp, do not put the bulb against the glass of the tank or the glass will break. We put the bulbs in a clamp-light reflector and hold the unit about an inch (2 cm) above the glass by affixing binder clips.

Another type of commercially available anole cage consists of a nylon mesh "skin" that fits around a take-apart tubular metal rectangular frame. A zipper closes the mesh cage along three sides of one end. The mesh sides provide vertical exploration space and maximum ventilation. We find this lightweight cage easy to take outside on a nice day, and with some adroit positioning to avoid melting the nylon mesh, we even use an incandescent UV light to provide heat and light when the cage is inside.

Some Terrarium Basics

1. We suggest that anoles be given the choice of as many and as varied perches as possible. Although the lizards will often position themselves head downward on vertical trunks, they also use diagonally or horizontally oriented perches, and smaller species sit atop broad leaves as well.

2. Illuminate and warm at least one of the horizontal perches (preferably two) from above, to provide a suitable area for thermoregulation. Branches of fruit trees or manzanita, if of suitable diameter, are ideal perch material.

3. Male anoles are territorial, but the females are usually compatible. Unless they are of diverse species, never try to keep more than a single male per cage. Visual barriers can be created by crisscrossing perches and properly positioning plants. Since the dominant specimen in any group will claim the most prominent and satisfactory basking spot, it is important to provide two or more additional areas conducive to your anoles' thermoregulation.

better, safer, and far more economical, after the initial purchase price, than single-glazed structures. There's a practical side to the double-glazed windows, as well. Since anoles often cling to the glass, the winter-frosted glass of single-pane construction can result in the loss of toes, feet, or even the death of the lizard. Greenhouses are usually considered permanent structures and a building permit is required to legally install one.

Security and Screening
Since anoles are talented escape artists, absolute security is essential. Vestibule-type double doors will help prevent escape. Additionally, heating and cooling units must be entirely screened from the inside to prevent injury to the inhabitants. It is important to screen even those fixtures well above ground level. The base of the greenhouse must be flush against a concrete slab, affixed to a concrete or brick

4. Anoles usually prefer to drink by lapping pendulous droplets of water from freshly misted plant leaves or bamboo sections. Unless the water surface is roiled with the bubbles from an aquarium airstone, driven by a small vibrator pump, many anoles will refuse to drink from a water dish.

5. Mist the leaves of your plants with tepid water daily. Be certain that your terrarium plants have not been freshly sprayed with insecticides or liquid fertilizers. Maintain commercially procured plants outside of the terrarium for a couple of weeks to allow systemic additives a chance to dissipate. Hose down the foliage twice a week to help rinse off sprayed insecticides and fertilizers.

6. Lighting is another consideration. Most plants, even those typically thought of as low-light species, will need strong lighting in order to grow well in a terrarium. Pothos and several species of bromeliads are among the hardiest and most attractive species that can do well with lower light levels. Incandescent fixtures using a commercial plant-grow floodlight bulb or a full-spectrum UV-B/heat bulb are ideal. These bulbs will provide warmth for your anoles as well as the needed illumination for the plants.

(stem) wall, or be sunk a foot (30 cm) or more below the surface of the ground. This will preclude easy access by outside predators and escape by the creatures with which you are working.

Interiors

It is important to provide the appropriate plantings, watering, heating, lighting systems, and cage furniture. The possibility and feasibility of providing a small pond and waterfall, often much-wanted accouterments, are entirely compatible with anole keeping. Well-planned ponds and waterfalls can be wonderful and feasible additions to a garden theme that would be impossible to construct in any other setting.

When approached with imagination and forethought, the interior of even a small greenhouse can become the focal point of your home and a wonderful home for your anoles.

Feeding and Watering Your Anoles

Fortunately, most of the anoles have rather easily duplicated diets. As a group, the lizards are primarily insectivorous, but they occasionally seek out nectar, pollen, exudates from overripe fruits, and hummingbird feeders. Larger anole species will also eat small vertebrates, including other lizards, and fruit.

Insects

Because anoles are preferentially insectivorous, it is these creatures that will form the bulk of the lizard's diet.

The size of the insects you provide must be determined by the size of your anoles. Four- or 5-inch-long (10–13 cm) anoles will best thrive on half-grown crickets or other insects of similar size. Anoles 8 inches (20 cm) long or larger will subsist perfectly well on adult crickets or other large insects. Hatchling and small juvenile anoles (of small species) will require a diet of pinhead-sized crickets or other tiny insects. Crickets of any size are available at most pet stores, or can be ordered by mail from cricket farms.

You must make sure that any insects being fed to the lizards are healthy and gut-loaded. (The technique of feeding your food insects a good diet before feeding them off goes by the descriptive but unappealing term of "gut-loading.") Using poorly fed insects cheats your anoles of much-needed nutrition. In contrast, a food insect that has fed on a variety of nutritious foods, particularly just before being offered as food to your insectivorous lizards, is a nutritional bonus package. Do keep in mind that insects will quickly lose much of their food value in only a few hours' time if not continually fed.

Jamaican giant anoles are strongly arboreal.

Dull when photographed here, *A. bahorucaensis southerlandi* of the Greater Antilles can be quite colorful when content.

Food for Insects

Foods to offer your feed insects include fresh fruit, grated carrots, squash, broccoli, fresh alfalfa and/or bean sprouts, honey, and chick laying mash, with calcium, vitamin D_3, and other vitamins added. Dampened chick laying mash, with a tiny pinch of vitamin/mineral supplement stirred in, is a good base diet, but a commercially prepared cricket gut-loading diet is also available. The manufacturer states that this food can be used for mealworms and king mealworms, too. Silkworms, food that many lizards seem to like a great deal, will require mulberry leaves or silkworm food. This comes as a powder or as a dark green ready-to-serve paste.

Types of Food Insects

Food insects that are commercially available include crickets, mealworms, giant mealworms, waxworms, houseflies, fruitflies, silkworms, and trevoworms (butterworms).

Where to Obtain Food Insects

If you need large numbers of food insects, get dealers' names and phone numbers from the classifieds in reptile magazines or check the World Wide Web. Web site vendors usually provide on-line ordering. If you need only small numbers of feed insects, your local pet or feed store may be your most economical source. Buying from your local pet or bait store has a distinct advantage over ordering quantities of food insects. You "instantly" have the insects you need, and you buy only the live insects; the store absorbs any losses from dead insects.

Field Plankton

Insects straight from the wild are already well fed. These insects have been able to choose their diet and their nutritive value reflects this. Field plankton is quite probably the very best diet that you can offer your anoles. It is merely a mixture of the various insects and arthropods that can be field collected in any given location. To gather them, you simply sweep a suitably meshed field net back and forth through tall grasses or low shrubs after first ascertaining that the area is insecticide free.

An Insect No-No

In some areas of the South large, slow locusts (grasshoppers) called "lubbers" can be found. Many of these have a brightly colored (often black and yellow or red) nymphal stage that is quite toxic and that can be fatal to your lizards if eaten. The tan and buff adults seem to be less toxic but their use as a food item is contraindicated.

Marketed under the invalid name of *A.* *"auriorum,"* nothing, including its true identity, is currently known about this anole.

anoles is important. Phosphorus acts as a calcium inhibitor. To attain benefit from supplemental dietary calcium, the phosphorus-calcium ratio must be 1:2. The provision of vitamin D_3 will assure that the calcium is metabolized.

Fruits and Exudates

Because many anoles readily lap up sweet fruit and exudates, this affords you a second simple way of administering the necessary vitamin and mineral supplements. Without these supplements, especially vitamin D_3 and calcium (but phosphorus also plays a significant role), the lizards may develop a metabolic bone disorder, once simply called "decalcification" or "rubber bone disease." Rapidly growing young and female anoles that are utilizing calcium to form shells for their developing eggs will be affected more quickly than adult males or nonovulating females (see the chapter on health for more information on this crippling disease).

Dietary Phosphorus Versus Calcium

The amount of dietary phosphorus versus calcium provided to your

Vitamins

An excess of vitamin D_3 can allow overmetabolizing of calcium and result in visceral and joint gout.

A diet deficient in vitamin A can cause eye and vision problems.

The prudent use of vitamin/mineral supplements is necessary, but care must always be used as they are administered. It takes only a pinch to provide what's needed.

The Role of UV Lighting

The effects of the ultraviolet wavelength UV-B, of vitamin D_3, of phosphorus, and of calcium are closely interrelated. UV-B promotes the natural synthesizing of previtamin D_3, which in turn allows the metabolism of calcium. Phosphorus can inhibit the proper utilization of calcium unless the amount of supplemental calcium given is at least twice that of the phosphorus.

When denied access to full-spectrum lighting, reptiles provided with dietary D_3 can metabolize calcium, but less effectively.

How to Make Fruit-Honey Mixture for Your Anoles

Mix

1/3 of a 4-ounce (112-g) jar of pureed papaya, apricot, or mixed fruit baby food

1 teaspoon of honey

1/4 eyedropper of Avitron liquid bird vitamins

1/2 teaspoon of Miner-All powdered reptile vitamins

Add enough water to make this mixture a soupy consistency.

A half tablespoon of bee pollen can be added if available.

Feed as needed in elevated dishes; refrigerate the portion that is not used, but discard and remake after one week.

Replace the mixture in the cage daily.

In nature, by basking extensively, heliothermic anoles synthesize the previtamin D_3 needed to fully utilize the available calcium. They benefit additionally from the wavelength UV-A that promotes natural behavior. Even shade-dwelling species, such as bearded chameleon anoles, benefit from reflected UV rays.

We can see, therefore, that full-spectrum lighting is very beneficial to reptiles. Although in lesser amounts than are available in unfiltered natural sunlight, these wavelengths may also be provided by artificial full-spectrum lighting, which is now available both in incandescent and fluorescent models.

When at all possible, we suggest that all three approaches—natural unfiltered sunlight (at least when weather permits), artificial full-spectrum lighting when the anoles are indoors, and dietary additives—be used. The additives are provided once weekly for most adult anoles and twice weekly for fast-growing babies and for females during the breeding season.

A word of caution: Since UV-B actually stimulates the synthesizing of D_3 when a high-quality UV-B emitting bulb or natural sunlight is provided, reduce the amounts of the D_3-calcium supplement. To date, there is no formula for determining the amount or frequency with which supplements should be provided. We can only urge that care be utilized.

The ghost anole, *A. angusticeps oligaspis*, is a denizen of the low trees on some of the Bahamian Islands.

A. trachyderma of Amazonian South America is called the common forest anole.

Watering

Providing adequate and suitable hydration for your anoles can be more of a challenge than providing a balanced diet. In the wild, anoles drink pendulous droplets that either fall or condense on leaves, twigs, or even their own bodies. Since these lizards often do not recognize quietly standing water as a drinking source, we mist the plants and branches in our indoor terraria daily, and the anoles are always ready to drink.

If you do decide to use a typical water dish for the anoles, roil the water's surface, as with a bubbling aquarium airstone, to make it recognizable to the lizards. Watch them to make certain they drink.

Outdoor cages can be gently sprinkled once or twice daily for a period of several minutes. Thirsty lizards drink copiously at these times.

A second, equally effective method of watering lizards outdoors is to place a large bucket with a few pinholes in the bottom on top of the top wire and over the plantings. When filled, the water drips slowly from the pinholes, splashing on the plantings and providing the lizards with a drinking source.

Veterinarians and Anoles

If they are properly fed, hydrated, and housed, anoles are relatively hardy and quite trouble-free. Yet even with the best of care, medical problems can arise, and some may require the assessment and intervention of a veterinarian. Regardless of their cost, anoles, like other animals, deserve the best care you can give them, and this care may include veterinary expenses. But be forewarned that not all veterinarians are comfortable treating reptiles, nor are all qualified to do so. We suggest that you find a suitable veterinarian before the need for one actually arises. Check the yellow pages of your local phone book, ask the veterinarian who treats your dog or cat for a referral, or check in the classified sections of reptile magazines for the reptile-qualified veterinarian closest to you. With access to the World Wide Web—public libraries can provide this to you at no charge—you can locate a reptile veterinarian by checking the veterinary membership of the Association of Reptile and Amphibian Veterinarians. Members are listed by state and by city.

Quarantine

To prevent the possible spread of diseases and parasites between anoles—most of which are collected from the wild—it is important that you quarantine new specimens for a period of time. Your new anole may arrive with a readily transmissible respiratory disease or other contagious illness, so avoid adding to your problems by quarantining your new lizards. A week would be the minimum quarantine

Its patchy brown and green coloration indicates that this green anole, *A. c. carolinensis*, is stressed.

time; a month is much better. During this time each quarantined anole should be in a cage by itself and you should be carefully cleaning/sterilizing your hands and any equipment you use between cages.

During quarantine, take the time just to watch your lizard. Make certain its behavior is normal, with no dragging of its hind limbs, spasmodic jerking of the head, or unseemly lethargy. The quarantine area should be completely separate from the area in which other reptiles are kept, ideally in a different room.

During the quarantine period, fecal samples should be examined to determine the parasite load. Some parasites may actually be beneficial in ways we don't yet understand. In green iguanas, nematodes, for instance, may help digestion by mechanically stirring up ingested food and also by breaking down the cellulose to a digestible form. To determine what's living in your anole's gut, take a fresh stool sample to your reptile veterinarian. The sample should not even be refrigerated before it is examined.

The quarantine cage should be thoroughly cleaned and sterilized—do not use cleansing agents containing phenols—prior to the introduction of the new lizard(s), and it should be regularly cleaned throughout the quarantine period. As with any other terrarium, the quarantine tank should be geared to the needs of the anole that it is to house. Temperature, humidity, size, lighting, and all other factors must be considered.

Only after you are completely satisfied that your new specimen(s) is healthy and habituated should it be brought into contact with other specimens.

Health Problems

Respiratory Ailments

Anoles are not particularly prone to respiratory ailments of any kind, but should one occur, it can quickly debilitate a choice specimen. Overly damp and cold shipping or caging conditions or other kinds of improper husbandry can trigger respiratory ailments. These can be viral or bacterial in origin and will require nasal or mucal swabs to determine the sensitivity of the causative agents to a particular medication. An anole suffering from a respiratory problem may display labored breathing through a partially opened mouth. While awaiting a medical opinion, elevate and maintain the cage temperature at 85 to 90°F (29–32°C) around the clock.

Mouth Rot

Infectious stomatitis is another malady that is seldom seen in anoles. It is caused by a secondary infection or bruises of the snout and mouth. If present, the soft tissue will be puffy, soft, and discolored, and a cheesy exudate may be present between the teeth. If untreated this can cause jawbone deterioration, tooth loss, and eventual death. Topical Neosporin and/or sulfa drugs, applied once or twice daily, are the medications of choice, but if a positive response is not quickly seen, consult your veterinarian. Loose exudate should be *gently* removed before each application of medication.

Broken Tail

Anoles occasionally lose or autotomize their tail. Although temporarily disfiguring, tail loss is a natural method of escaping predators. Areas in the tail vertebrae, called fracture planes, break if the tail is restrained and the anole does not stop. Tail loss is not a health threat and tail regeneration will occur.

Metabolic Bone Disease

MBD is an insidious disease that is caused by improper nutrition, specifically by too little dietary calcium or, if calcium is present in suitable amounts, by the inability of the lizard to metabolize it properly. Briefly, MBD occurs when calcium is taken from the bones of the anole to maintain calcium levels in the blood. As a result, the bones are shortened and weakened. In the longer bones, as in the leg bones, fibrous tissue grows around them to help support them. Visible symptoms include a shortened, puffy jawline, chubby-looking legs while the animal's body is thin, and leg and vertebral bones that break under what seems to be normal day-to-day use. The role of ultraviolet light, vitamin D_3, and calcium is discussed in detail on page 32. A veterinarian can help diagnose MBD, but in the meantime, add a powdered vitamin/mineral supplement (look for both vitamin D_3 and calcium) to the food insect and food nectar.

Stress

Anoles that are kept too cool, too crowded, too hot, or subjected to aggression by dominant terrarium mates will display certain signs of stress. Among these are a tendency for the subordinate specimen(s) to continually hide, to lack a feeding response, to be continually fearful and nervous, and to persistently display an abnormal coloration (usually dark). Stress can eventually prove fatal to an otherwise healthy anole. Observe your lizards frequently and get to know what are, for yours, normal colors and responses. Do not mix sizes. Stress may be reduced by adding visual barriers, by placing your animals in a larger cage, by adjusting cage temperature, or by adding additional females. If, after all of these corrective measures, stress continues, you will have no choice but to separate your specimens into individual terraria. If this becomes necessary, it is usually possible to periodically move the male to the female's container for the purpose of breeding. Watch carefully for signs of overt aggressiveness toward the female by the male. It may be necessary to again separate the two almost immediately. If relatively compatible it still may be necessary to again separate the two after breeding has been accomplished. Observe and be ready to take whatever steps are necessary.

Skin Shedding

All lizards shed their skin. Shedding occurs with more frequency during periods of fast growth or to repair skin damage. Shedding is the result of thyroid activity. As the old keratinous layer loosens from the new one forming beneath it, your anole may dull considerably in color for a day or more. When shedding has been completed your specimen will brighten up.

Although it seems that wild anoles seldom have problems shedding, some captives may. Shedding problems may often be associated with specimens that are dehydrated or in otherwise suboptimal condition, or when the relative humidity in the terrarium/cage is too low.

Shedding problems are most often associated with narrow areas

The blue-fronted anole, *A. allisoni*, a species of Belize and Cuba, is one of the most beautiful of these variable lizards.

if your anole is dropped, if it falls, or even if it jumps from a moderate height. These injuries can also occur if the anole is trapped beneath or in back of a shifting piece of heavy cage furniture. Improper calcium metabolization or MBD will increase the likelihood of such a problem. If severe enough to be at all debilitating, veterinary assessment should be sought immediately. Your veterinarian may recommend either strapping the broken limb to the side of the anole until the break can heal or euthanasia.

such as toes and tail tips. Although anoles are adept at removing these problematic pieces themselves, if they do not succeed, their keeper must intervene very carefully. Leaving dried skin in place can result in toe or tail tip loss. If patches of skin adhere, a gentle misting with tepid water or a daub of mineral oil from a cotton swab may help make its manual removal easier.

Skin Infections

Skin infections are not common, but may occur if an anole's terrarium is too humid or allowed to foul. Correct husbandry will negate this problem. Clean the cage, throwing out the old substrate and thoroughly cleaning the sides and bottom of the cage. Replace or clean/boil any cage furniture that can take that sort of treatment. A topical antibiotic powder, sprinkled onto the skin lesions, may help speed the healing process.

Physical Injuries

Broken limbs and other physical injuries can (but usually won't) occur

Parasites

Although anoles do not seem particularly plagued by endoparasites, some may harbor these pests. Heavy loads of endoparasites may cause bloody stools or other intestinal discomfort. Because of the complexities of identification of endoparasites and the necessity to accurately weigh specimens to be treated and measure purge dosages, the treatment of internal parasites is best left to a qualified reptile veterinarian. It is important to use the correct medications and correct dosages. Because of the small size of the patient, there is no room for error.

Ectoparasites such as ticks and mites are seldom a problem. Ticks, which are quite large, may be removed with tweezers. Rotate the tick to loosen and remove the mouthparts. Mites, which on lizards usually congregate on the sides of the neck or around the limbs and tail base, may be eradicated by coating them with mineral oil or dilute Ivermectin solution. Once dead, they will drop off.

Breeding

Despite the fact that few are bred in captivity, it is not difficult to cycle anoles reproductively. It would seem that interest in breeding and the formation of viable sperm—spermatogenesis—in male anoles is triggered by photoperiod, the naturally occurring hours of daylight versus darkness. It is probable that other cues are also important, especially in equatorial species where there is little seasonal change in day length. Ovulation by the females is probably dependent upon natural cues, but is also actually caused by the courtship display of one or more males.

All anoles are oviparous, reproducing by laying eggs. Most small species lay only a single egg at a time; some large species may lay several. Several clutches, of single or multiple eggs, are produced each season, usually at 14- to 21-day intervals.

One of the greatest thrills and challenges for those of us who maintain reptiles is to find and develop the keys necessary to breed the creatures successfully. Fortunately, most anoles respond well to captive conditions, are easy to sex, and, once acclimated, most are not hesitant to breed. We'll describe the process for green and brown anoles; the same process applies to most of the other species.

Anole Reproduction

The criteria for inducing anole reproduction are simple. Provide a natural photoperiod, an adequate diet with ample vitamin and mineral additives, suitable caging (including space, temperature, lighting, security, and an egg-deposition site), and make sure that both sexes of anoles are present.

It may take anoles several weeks to acclimate to captive conditions. However, once they have become accustomed to their surroundings and have staked out their territories, breeding may occur throughout the spring months and well into the summer.

The male anole usually grasps the female by the nape of the neck during breeding.

This hatchling large-headed anole is from the Miami population.

Hatchling knight anoles, *A. e. equestris*, are usually some shade of brown, often with a greenish tinge, and have white crossbands.

Sexually mature male anoles have a swollen tail base and a distensible dewlap. Females have a narrow tail base, and if a dewlap is present, it is proportionately smaller than that of the male.

From late spring throughout the summer, the female anole lays a single egg at fortnight intervals. Each incidence of ovarian development is stimulated by a courtship sequence. Since sperm can be stored in viable condition for periods exceeding eight months, actual copulation prior to each egg deposition is not essential.

Nests

If a nest is prepared, it is a rather haphazard affair. It may consist only of a shallow scraped ditch in a moist spot, only slightly deeper than the diameter of the egg. As often as not, the parchment-shelled egg is merely laid in leaf litter, amid trash heaps, or in similar moisture-retaining sites.

A leafy terrarium substrate forms a perfectly acceptable deposition site for captive anoles.

Incubation

Incubation averages two months. It may be somewhat less in hot weather, somewhat greater if climatic conditions are cool. Hatchlings are relatively large, often exceeding 2 inches (5 cm) in total length.

Anole eggs can be easily incubated. Temperatures between 78 and 86°F (25–30°C)—80 to 84°F (26–29°C) is best—and a high humidity are needed. We suggest an incubation medium of either fine vermiculite or sphagnum moss. This must be moistened to a proper consistency and kept at a suitable temperature. We use an inexact but simple way of determining the proper moisture content of the incubation medium: Moisten it thoroughly, then squeeze it as dry as possible in your tightened fist.

occur during incubation, or even as the full-term young are trying to break from their eggs.

Hatching

At the end of the incubation period, which may vary in duration from 30 to about 70 days, the baby anoles will pip. The eggs of larger species take longer to develop than those of small species. For example, the eggs of green anoles, brown anoles, bark anoles, and crested anoles often hatch in 30 to 40 days, while those of Jamaican giant anoles and knight anoles have been known to incubate between 55 and 67 days. Plan on having tiny food insects on hand when the babies emerge from the eggs.

The babies may remain in the pipped egg for several hours, or may emerge almost immediately. Once they have hatched they should be moved to another terrarium and offered food, a sunning spot, and water. Their postnatal shed should occur from several hours to a few days after hatching.

Anolis pulchellus is one of the Puerto Rican grass anoles.

Depending on the species of your anole and the temperature at which the eggs are incubated, the incubation duration will usually be between four and six weeks.

Anole eggs do not have rigidly calcified shells. Carefully move the eggs from the terrarium. Try to retain the position in which they are lying. Place each egg on the barely moistened substrate in the incubator.

Check the temperature daily and add a little water to the incubating medium as needed. The preferred humidity is 80 to 90 percent.

A saturated atmosphere, where the moisture condenses and drips onto the eggs, is not desirable. The medium of vermiculite or perlite should be damp to the touch but sufficiently dry so that water cannot be squeezed out by hand. Do not wet the eggs when you are remoistening the medium.

Infertile eggs will discolor and will usually collapse. If you are certain the eggs are infertile, they may be removed and discarded. For any number of reasons, embryo death may

The male banded tree anole is obscurely banded, a pretty green, and has a huge yellow dewlap.

Making Your Own
Anole Egg Incubator

Materials needed for one incubator:
1 wafer thermostat/heater (obtainable from feed stores; these are commonly used in incubators for chicks)
1 thermometer
1 styrofoam cooler—one with thick sides (a fish-shipping box is ideal)
1 heat tape
1 heavy wire shelf to hold egg containers an inch or two (2–5 cm) above the coiled heat tape
3 wire nuts

Your goal is to wire the thermostat between the heat tape and the electrical cord (see below) in order to regulate the amount of heat produced by the heat tape.

1. Cut some of the electrical cord off the heat tape, leaving about 18 inches (46 cm) of the cord on the heat tape. Make a hole through the side of the styrofoam box, about 5 inches (13 cm) below the top edge. Pull the separated electrical cord through the hole, leaving the plug end outside (don't plug it in just yet!). Strip off about 1/2 inch (1 cm) of the insulation from the wiring at the cut end, and separate the two wires by a few inches.

2. Coil the heat tape loosely in the bottom of the box, making sure that it doesn't cross over itself at any point. Coil the tape so that the recently cut end is near the electrical cord.

3. Using one of the wire nuts, connect one of the red wires of the thermostat to one of the electrical wires of the heat tape. Use a second nut to connect the second red wire of the thermostat to one of the wires of the electrical cord. Use the third nut to connect the second wire of the electrical cord to the second wire of the heat tape, in effect reestablishing part of the original wiring between the heat tape and its electrical cord.

4. Put the lid on the cooler, and plug in the thermostat/heater. Wait half an hour and check the temperature. The L-shaped pin on the top of the thermostat is the rheostat; turn it to increase or decrease the temperature inside your new incubator. You want the inside to be 80 to 86°F (26–30°C).

Once you have the temperature regulated, add your hardware cloth "shelf," and put the container of eggs on top of the shelf. Close the egg container.

Check the temperature daily and add a little water to the incubating medium if it gets dry; it should stay damp enough to stick together when you stick your finger into it, or when you push it into a little heap with your finger. Take care to add the water to the medium, not onto the eggs. The preferred humidity is 80 to 90 percent. Placing an open deli container, half filled with water, onto the hardware cloth shelf will also help maintain the humidity.

Glossary

Agonistic: Antagonistic, hostile.

Ambient temperature: The temperature of the surrounding environment.

Anterior: Toward the front.

Anus: The external opening of the cloaca; the vent.

Arboreal: Tree dwelling.

Autotomize: The ability to break easily, or to voluntarily cast off (and usually to regenerate) a part of the body, such as the tail.

Caudal: Pertaining to the tail.

Cloaca: The common chamber into which digestive, urinary, and reproductive systems empty and that itself opens exteriorly through the vent or anus.

Deposition: As used here, the laying of the eggs.

A. limifrons of Central America is small, slender, and lacks bright colors.

Deposition site: The spot chosen by the female to lay her eggs or have young.

Dewlap (also called throat or gular fan): A voluntarily distensible fan of skin on the throats of anoles. This is either missing or comparatively small on females.

Dimorphic: A difference in form, build, or coloration involving the same species; often sex linked.

Diurnal: Active in the daytime.

Dorsal: Pertaining to the back; upper surface.

Dorsolateral: Pertaining to the upper sides.

Dorsum: The upper surface.

Ecological niche: The precise habitat utilized by a species.

Ectothermic: Cold-blooded.

Endothermic: Warm-blooded.

Form: An identifiable species or subspecies.

Genus: A taxonomic classification of a group of species having similar characteristics. The genus falls between the next higher designation of family and the next lower designation of species. Genera is the plural of genus. A genus name is always capitalized when written.

Gravid: The reptilian equivalent of mammalian pregnancy.

Gular: Pertaining to the throat.

This male *A. lineatopus*, a species indigenous to Jamaica, is in an aggressive stance.

Heliothermic: Pertaining to a species that basks in the sun to thermoregulate.

Hemipenes: The dual copulatory organs of male lizards and snakes.

Hemipenis: The singular form of hemipenes.

Herpetoculture: The captive breeding of reptiles and amphibians.

Herpetoculturist: One who indulges in herpetoculture.

Herpetologist: One who indulges in herpetology.

Herpetology: The study (often scientifically oriented) of reptiles and amphibians.

Hibernation: A period of winter dormancy.

Hydrate: To restore body moisture by drinking or absorption.

Juvenile: A young or immature specimen.

Labial: Pertaining to the lips.

Lateral: Pertaining to the side.

Middorsal: Pertaining to the middle of the back.

Midventral: Pertaining to the center of the belly or abdomen.

Nuchal crest: A crest, often voluntarily erectile, on the nape of the neck.

Oviparous: Reproducing by means of eggs that hatch after laying.

Photoperiod: The daily/seasonally variable length of the hours of daylight.

Polychrotines: Lizards of the family Polychrotidae; anoles and relatives.

Race: A subspecies.

Setae: The microscopic hairlike bristles in the subdigital lamallae of an anole's toes.

Species: A group of similar creatures that produce viable young when breeding; the taxonomic designation that falls beneath genus and above subspecies; abbreviation: sp.

Subdigital lamellae: the transverse plates (grooves and ridges) that extend across the undersurface of an anole's toes.

Subspecies: The subdivision of a species; a race that may differ slightly in color, size, scalation, or other criteria; abbreviation: ssp.

Taxonomy: The science of classification of plants and animals.

Thermoregulate: To regulate (body) temperature by choosing a warmer or cooler environment.

Vent: The external opening of the cloaca; the anus.

Venter: The underside of a creature; the belly.

Ventral: Pertaining to the undersurface or belly.

Ventrolateral: Pertaining to the sides of the venter (belly).

Helpful Information

Herpetological societies (or clubs) exist in major cities in North America, Europe, and other areas of the world. All such clubs welcome inquiries and new members. Two of the professional herpetological societies are:

Society for the Study of Amphibians
    and Reptiles (SSAR)
Department of Zoology
Miami University
Oxford, OH 45056

Herpetologist's League
c/o Texas National Heritage Program
Texas Parks and Wildlife Department
4200 Smith School Road
Austin, TX 78744

The SSAR publishes two quarterly journals: *Herpetological Review*

contains husbandry, range extensions, news on ongoing field studies, and so forth, whereas the *Journal of Herpetology* contains articles more oriented toward academic herpetology.

Hobbyist magazines for herpetology and herpetoculture (including lizards) are:

Reptiles
P.O. Box 6050
Mission Viejo, CA 92690

Reptile and Amphibian Hobbyist
One TFH Plaza
Neptune City, NJ 07753

The hobbyist magazines also carry classified ads and news about herp expos.

Index